MW01169217

2019   Volume XXXIII

Managing Editors	ELLEN SUMMERS
	JANET SUMMERS
Poetry Editors	RACHELLE M. PARKER
	ELLEN SUMMERS
	JAN HAAG
Prose Editor	JANET SUMMERS
Emerging Voices Editor	KAREN BUCHINSKY
Layout	LANE GODDARD
Publisher	PAT SCHNEIDER

ISBN: 1694298485
ISBN 13: 978-1694298485
ISSN: 0890-622x

Amherst Writers & Artists Press, Inc.
P.O. Box 1076
Amherst, MA 01004
Phone: 413 253 3307

peregrine@amherstwriters.org
www.amherstwriters.org

Peregrine is published annually. Submission details are available at amherstwriters.org or peregrinejournal.submittable.com. Payment is in copies. The editors endorse the practice of simultaneous submissions.

Copies are available on Amazon.com for $12.

Amherst Writers & Artists (AWA) affiliates offer writing workshops for adults, youth, and children across the world. In addition, AWA sponsors public readings and maintains an international training program that supports the work of writers and artists. Amherst Writers & Artists Press, Inc., publishes *Peregrine*, books of poetry and fiction, and the Amherst Writers & Artists poetry chapbook series.

Cover art by Barry Moser (used with permission)
Peregrine nesting sketch by Karen Buchinsky (used with permission)

CONTENTS

DEVON MILLER-DUGGAN

Some Women, Some Children, Some Rivers
After James Wright

They have come gladly out of the willows.
Willows reach into rivers,
catch the bodies of women who
give themselves to the water.
That is how they are found and known
in stories where they've loved unwisely.
Wild things and whips the branches make,
nets, crowns, baskets, nooses, lures.
The trees themselves call lightning for love:
see how they branch themselves, mimicking
light needing to touch the ground.
Everything needs ground to fall toward.
Everything needs a hiding place and
no hiding place is always safe; therefore
the willows weep, knowing
the danger of their roots weaving
the edges of running water.

Children live there, in stories,
safer than in houses or under skies,
and come gladly, or cannot,
bound as they are
by branches. And lightning comes
gladly, changed before it changes.

Cartography of a Name

Before I learn the strokes to my name,
I begin from the basics.

A Sunday morning spent in school and
I could tell you the difference of curvature

between small and big: hook of a woman's
crossed legs against a man's spread feet.

Wait a week, and I could stack words
like legos to build meaning.

I could tell you life is water/dirt/cavity,
that every home requires a roof and a pig,

and the sky is only a synthesis
of one and big.

A year later, when I've sufficiently
learned every organ of vocabulary

I grasp my name. The parts of each word:
thousand, teeth, grassland.

I punctuate every component with
a satisfaction until I realize I do not know

what grass and labor, teeth and man
mean together compounded, and even worse

I do not know what my full name
is trying to say.

But now it's after forgetting the
basics, what I don't want to say

is that there is only one
phrase left I understand:

外国人 foreigner

Kathrynn Axton-Roosevelt

Poverty

children sign
      fingers cocked sideways,
      exaggerated screams

urban mother's sigh,
hopeful their sons grow
without expiration dates
memorialized
          on concrete walls.

Fairy Tale Lessons

For the good girl that still believes in fairy tales,
you must use your imagination
if you want them to come true.
For your Prince Charming is not coming,
he's at home taking a nap.
Your son Jack ran away with the gold coins
and your friend Robin Hood is in jail.
You must use your own magic,
especially when the wolf comes to destroy your house.
Sprinkle gold dust, flash your big, sharp, white teeth, and grab the
    longbow.
If all of that fails, then invite the wolf in for milk and gingerbread
    cookies.
Hansel and Gretel are already waiting.

Mariner

I'm awake again. Gasping, choking, arms flailing, hands reaching out for purchase against the buried tree roots and crumbling dirt of that slope that isn't there. My eyes are wide open and the smell of damp earth and stagnant water in my nostrils is so strong it's painful. I'm not crying though. Not this time. Sometimes I wake up screaming. Tonight, I was just trying to get back up the cliff, to escape his grip before he dragged me under with him. He couldn't get his seatbelt off and he was panicking as the car sank into the pond. He grabbed at my ankles as I swam past to reach the closest slope. He managed a good hold on one of them and I turned around, trying to free myself. I could barely see him through the tea-colored water. I saw his mouth open, bubbles pouring out, and his eyes. The whites of his eyes stood out against the muddy background and seemed to exist by themselves there, hanging in the water column. I was running out of air. I kicked to loosen his grip and I felt my foot connect with his face. Then I was swimming, crawling, clawing toward the surface and to the steep banks. I pulled myself up, slipping a few times in the process, until I found a sturdy exposed tree root to hold on to. I was gasping and watching in disbelief as the car disappeared below the surface and bubbles slowly stopped emerging. The sun had set behind the hill and cast the pond in shadow. Somehow, I mustered up the courage to go back and see if I could get him out. As I swam toward the bottom, my hands groping blindly for the car, I knew he was dead. I bumped against the roof and felt my way along the side until I got to the driver's door. I reached in the window and felt the cotton of his sweatshirt, swollen with water. There was no movement when I touched him. I reached over him, groping for the button for the seatbelt. He had buckled it into the wrong hole, that's why he couldn't get out. I pushed down the button and the seatbelt whizzed past me, the stream of bubbles caressing my face as they passed by. I swam for the surface, knowing I didn't have enough air to do this and pull him out. Managing a hitching deep breath, I submerged again and swam, arms in front of me, feeling for the side of the car. When I made contact with the driver's side mirror, I was startled when his arm floated out the window and brushed by me. I grabbed his arm and shook it, some part of my brain somehow thinking he was alive after much too long without air. There was nothing but bubbles. I pulled him out of the window and tried to swim to the surface, holding the hood of his sweatshirt in one hand and flailing my arms and legs. It was so much work and it felt like I was hardly moving. I was just about to let go when I felt my hand break the surface. The promise of air was enough to propel me the rest of the way and I dragged him as far out of the water as I could. His eyes and mouth were still open, frozen in the panic of his final moments. I screamed at him as steam rose from our bodies into the cool night air.

I missed his funeral because I was still in the ICU. That was 25 years ago. I still dream about that night at least a few times a month, more often if I'm stressed. The irony of these night terrors is that I was planning on killing him myself. Not like it ended up happening, I was going to make it much less traumatic for him, but still. What kind of potential murderer ends up getting traumatized when their victim dies but not by the method they had planned? Amateur. Of course, I never told anyone this. They had me go to so many counselors and therapists and psychologists. Countless interviews, evaluations, medications. They had no idea. And I was, am, genuinely disturbed by my experience, it's not like I was faking the panic attacks and meltdowns and survivor's guilt. But the fact still remains that I had a plan and that plan was derailed when we slid off the road that night. I remember clearly the very last thought I had before waking up in the hospital. As I watched the steam rise from his face, forever frozen in terror, I thought of the end of a verse from a book I read in school when I was very young. "And a thousand, thousand slimy things lived on. And so did I."

The Bats of Waugh Bridge
In the aftermath of Hurricane Harvey, 2017

They slept all day as the waters rose. They sensed its closeness when
   they woke—
yet what else could they do but what they'd always done:

letting go
headfirst
into the air
trusting
the drop
once more
to allow
them time
to change
direction

to turn
to rise

to open their wings, to catch themselves—

Rain Dance

I remember the first time he wrapped his hands around my throat.
They shook as if Jesus were calling and he put him through to
   voicemail.
Words ejected from his mouth, covered in spit or venom--on mute.
Images clicked, one by one, just behind my eyes.
A blue sky, a cloud in the shape of a frog, a drop of rain
diving head first into the desert.
The droplet regains its wobbly shape in a drunken, dust-covered
   dance.
I want to touch it, hold it, drink it, but it flattens into the scorched
   earth,
escaping me. Black-red pulsing eyes sear flesh, scar bone, carve
   initials:
True Love Forever.
No water, no Jesus, just two crying babies and a mortgage for a house
made of glass and wrapped in cellophane.
A jolt of hot electricity gives me goosebumps and makes
the back of my neck, the backs of my knees, the tip of each finger
   tingle.
Medusa's garden blooms in Lancaster, Ohio, and I turn to stone
   beneath his grip.
Smooth polished granite with speckles of peach and black.
The shimmer of mica scattered like freckles under my skin.
The granite is cold and hard, causing his hands to cramp and fall away.
He looks at his watch and decides to make a sandwich.

1969

They would have been sitting at
their kitchen table, I've decided,
she with some slippery fabric that
spilled out of her lap onto
the painfully white tiled floor
and stained the walls with black and blue blood.
(My grandmother has always been good with her hands.)

He would have been talking excitedly, I've decided,
about some political rally or a play he was writing,
his hands flailing like horseflies
and his spit flecked with Yiddishisms.
(This is before my grandfather lost some of his fine motor skills
and wore his meals like war decoration.)

There would have been a pause in his speech, I've decided,
and she, with the way she could instill drama
with the point of a needle, would have quietly spoken up and said,
"I am carrying someone else's child."

I have not decided what happens next. Maybe
he stands up and walks away,
his footsteps on the tile like
plates crashing against the wall.
(She likes to throw dishes when she's angry.)

What happens next,
at some point or another,
(and this is not what I have decided
but pure and simple fact)
is that he decides to stay.

In Between Skins

Ghost Crab,
Ocypode Quadrata
Sand shifting
my pentagon of body
bulging
legs wiring—we don't
belong
our heart
blooms too large for
our skin
we outgrow our shape—
we become
shell rising
transposing from vital to
unnecessary
an exoskeleton we leave
behind
thin-skinned
in this biome made for clams,
sharks—
creatures with hard shells, sharp
teeth
soft-shelled
scuttling, scrambling
vulnerable
we scrape, we scarcely
survive

Sweet and Sour

The mirror never lies. Rosa has never been beautiful, but today her reflection reveals another bitter truth. Death is chasing her.

She yearns for her homeland on the rugged coast hugging the Bay of Naples. The longing starts in her toes, creeping up through aging bones, searching, probing, until it finds her fragile heart, leaving it bare.

Rosa sees again the village of her childhood where the misty spring rain cloaked the houses in a blanket of gray, the roar and hiss of wintry waves gnawed at the cliffs, and all over the hillsides, the scent of lemons ripening in the sun infused the air. The aroma so reminiscent of her family's lemon groves where the chestnut wood trellises were repeated row upon row reaching far up the mountainside. Her hand remembers the warm breath of the mule as she guided him along the steep terraces, wicker baskets on his back laden with fertilizer for Papà to feed the trees. Rosa's withering mouth thirsts for the taste of those sweet, juicy lemons.

She conjures a last supper of her favorite foods: sardines caught fresh from the bay served oven-baked with a generous squeeze of lemon and parsley; icy cold lemon sorbet so refreshing in the sultry heat; and the melt-in-the-mouth lemon cake like her mother used to make.

Rosa touches her trembling lips and feels again the tenderness of her first kiss with Paolo stolen in a silken summer sea, and all the promise that kiss held for their future.

She weeps when she recalls the unraveling. Lives lost in the Second World War—Papà, her brother Guido and her beloved Paolo. Her hands find her stomach and she is haunted by the memory of the excruciating pain. Blood. So much blood. She grieves anew for the baby that was never to be. Quiet tears becoming loud, wailing sobs. There was no escaping the aftermath. The sharp sting of her mother's hand on her cheek and the shame of the words: "You bring disgrace on the family." Her mother sending her into exile to an alien shore at the bottom of the world to marry a countryman she had never met and could not find the passion to love.

She stares at her reflection again. The mark of her dead husband, Alfredo, is etched into every line and misshapen bone on her face.

The beatings when he was drunk, when he lost money playing cards, and every time another baby slipped away from her body in silence. "A defective bitch," he called her. Still they tried for that elusive thing called happiness. There was nowhere else to go.

Now Rosa is an old woman and there will be no one to mourn her passing. It will be as if she never existed, here in this sunburnt land with its unpredictable rains and empty soil. A place of such sour, disappointing lemons.

Autumn in Florida (B Side)

"Remember, green's your color. You are Spring." – Gwendolyn Brooks,
from "To The Young Who Want to Die"

The rest of the world bursts with color. I am evergreen. Cooler weather is not coming, so I decide when. When is always the question. When is your next appointment, Danny asks. He is Summer. He still waits for September. When does it get less miserable? I gave up so long ago. It is ninety degrees today. Climatologists say autumn is disappearing across the nation, summer slipping its warm tongue straight into winter. It almost makes Florida feel less alone. My mother tells me it snowed in Sarasota in '87, or maybe '88. Perhaps I, too, am capable of such unfathomable change. I have never seen a snowfall. I have never seen the trees blush. When I decide it is time for the undressing of leaves, I shrug off my coat and I call it Autumn.

Think Berlin

Wall them out,
the enemies
who reap our crops for us,
who sweep our houses clean,
who mind our babies.
Wall them out and tell

our fathers and our fathers' fathers
that they don't belong.
Turn back our mothers' boats
to war, to famine,
to the burning stake.
Lady Liberty steps down

and throws her torch
in New York Harbor
where it sizzles and goes out.
She jumps in after it
and disappears.
Not until we weep

a critical mass of tears
will we be floated
high and over walls,
the walls designed
to keep the other out,
the walls that keep us in.

Fall, 1925

In this one you wear
a fur coat, skunk, black and white.
You are a modern young woman.
It is late fall, 1925.

The car is a Nash
with a fancy radiator cap,
a valve-in-head motor
and hydraulic brakes.

The dapper man
is your husband in a
leather jacket and a blue shirt.
You are back from Niagara Falls.

The war to end all wars is over.
Family feuds are settled.
You are Wisconsin dairy farmers.
The future is open.

Hitler is still a young man in the old country.

Catherine

"Don't leave me this way...." This was my jam. I have been saying "good bye" to folks all my life. Not sure where I came from. I was just passed from hand to hand to house to house, just like a bad penny. I'd turn up in the strangest of places. After old Uncle Buddy died, I was moved again for the seventh time or was it the eighth time?

At thirteen years old I moved in with Cousin Kate. Who informed me that I was to call her Sister Mother Catherine and never ever anything else.

You see, Sister Mother, the good Catherine, was one of those saints who gets on a crowded subway train and commences to hollering and yelling, "Jesus, forgive them for they know not what they have done...." She would dress in clerical clothes. But she was still big and beautiful. You could see her pretty, folded up on hold, behind her passion for the word. I went with her one time. Her voice drowned out the noise of the speeding train. She said that it was up to me whether to accompany her, and after that one time of passing my hat for "Jesus," that was it for me; you should have seen the looks I got from people.

Sister Mother Catherine and I slept in the same bed sometimes. Weird, right? Without warning she would just climb in and say, "Shimmy over." She would tell me stories until I fell off to sleep. She didn't sweeten them up at all; I thought she would have on account of my age and all. But, she only knew how to tell the true, and nothing but.

It turns out that Sister Mother Catherine was the best home out of all my homes. We cooked together and even read the good book from cover to cover. Sister Mother Catherine had a way of explaining the Bible that tickled my funny bone something awful. And I wasn't allowed to giggle or wiggle in my seat or nothing. So, I took to yawning to hide a belly laugh when she interpreted the scripture. It was something about the way she said, "Beware and heed the raft of the Lord." She said it over and over, even during the happy parts.

One night she climbed into bed with me—did I say it was a tiny bed? The funny thing was that I had never had any skin on skin closeness before, not knowing my parents and all. I started to look forward to her warm round body pushed close to mine. It was like an anchor of sorts.

She was a sweet woman, but parts of her mind were younger than mine. Over time, she gave me a tiny piece of her life in stories. She vowed never to marry. No man would come between her and the Lord again. It was like a serial; every couple of nights I'd learn a little more. Only the story got sad. It was more about revenge and using the Lord to cover up her sins. She slowly confessed that she had done away with her pastor many years ago. "A filthy snake if there ever was one." He had deflowered her. By the time she figured out where things were headed, when she realized the pastor was made of flesh, it was too late; he was already bearing down on her.

She cried and said, "I would have followed that man to hell and back, so I just wasn't thinking that he might just be nasty and do that to me. I was nineteen and pure. But beware and heed the raft of the Lord."

Only he and her and her Lord knows what "done away with" means. She looked at me sideways and never did tell me that part.

Over the years she continued to witness and yell out warnings on crowded subways. I didn't tell her secrets to a living soul because I wanted to stay with her always. She was the best home I had ever had.

Before the Kinsey Scale

The synchronized fluttering of their midair copulation
mimics the elegant one-two steps in ballroom dancing.
Gender makes no difference to the wasps,
or maybe their brains can't make the connection,
but either way I am curious how we compare.

An emotional and chemical rush
(or is it just experimentation)
leading us from person to person
like pissed off martians on the attack.
At each stop of the journey we leave an X
on the map of our gendered identity,
with the sum showing us who we are.

Or am I the only wasp among men?

For My Father

The house sinks, splintering, and the birds
notice. There, song is counter-intuitive,
a song realized by its end note.
The light hits Lincoln Street the same this
April. She left the window open.
Teddy, get your shoes.
Remember her voice? How it loved you?
We'll take the bus to the Athenaeum today
instead of walking. We're running late. Teddy?
Teddy, don't be silly. Put on your Sunday shoes.
What am I going to do when you grow up?
Come here and kiss me, my perfect little man.
Promise me you'll never grow up.
A sirocco shrieks from the wilderness
sucking the breath out of you.
Calm down, calm down a voice floats
outside of you but you know
you are dying, and you are not calm.

Haikus on Hyphens

Life as a hyphen:
Dash of each and fully none.
Blank-American.

Life is a hyphen
if Cuban-Americans
are too much of each.

Life is a hyphen
if Cuban-Americans`
lack a pinch of each.

There is no hyphen,
for Cuban Americans
are more than enough.

Fear

Sitting in this dark place, in this jagged corner. Hearing the music of my past-- the tenor, he's Irish, that's what would be believed. Remembering Momma in church, her gold bracelets clang as she spins the prayer wheel, while her amethyst eyes, beautiful as ever, shine bright when she smiles. Then we would go home for supper. She would cook what we always ate, lentil soup, the ladle dripping, pulling it out, dividing it between the five of us. The dripping ladle will then be cleaned for morning porridge. We are no longer able to be visible, we hide underground for fear of the chant, that chant is rising, loudly proclaiming they are looking for us. Momma tells me to grab my younger brother for he is slow. The boy is terrified they have found us. I place in his hands the lollipop that was being saved, the one that will save us. Momma's silk undergarments on the clothesline float on the wind. Younger brother squeals at it. Momma rushes to run cover his mouth. The lollipop will have to tide him over. I silently pray we will cross the bridge that will send us to freedom, as we hear the bellow of the shotgun in the air. The hair on the back of my neck prickles in fear. The bolt hit the side of the house when they shot.

Disney Dwarf

I want to live as a Disney Dwarf, sing each
morning on my way to work our mine, after
a spirited evening with the lovely Snow.

After swinging my pick and chanting wishes
for riches, wearing simple Technicolor tunic,
I want contained conversations with family
and one good sitcom friend, whose daughter

made a gingerbread house, all red frosting
splattered over snow & trees & shrubs, a dead
Santa, decapitated snowman, incompetent
cops, and we just laugh it off, hang

our picks on the rack by the door, refill
steins with a bemused, "heigh ho,"
gorge ourselves on mass-produced pizzas,
and settle in to watch laugh track Dwarf TV,
so grateful to enjoy our
unexamined lives of plenty today.

Three Nightscapes

I. The Garden

An enchantress sighs in the room you thought empty, clearing a place for you. She calls out, this seductive crone, in a language you almost recall. She needs to remind you of something, but you have no way to respond beyond the ghost-like assent of your presence. Beyond the barking of the dogs, below the level of speech is a place that grants access, so you enter. She carries a lifetime of pain and loss. Hers is an unassailable grief that finds release in the few remaining joys left to her—calling birds down from the trees and feeding them from the palm of her hand, bathing throughout the moonlit night in the tropical garden, loving the humid air that pours the essence of jasmine, lemongrass and nightshade across the ravaged contours of her flesh, a white cat the sole witness to the forms she takes in her purposeful flight from pure earth to pure light. Miracles arise into this nightscape, where pride cannot withstand the onslaught of beauty. Your limbs grow heavy and descend earthward. Your mouth gnaws the earth in murmurs of longing, ensconced in this woman's garden where she paints herself into her surroundings, where she paints herself into the light and the darkness.

II. The Lake/The Forest

Where are the people? Where is your tribe? Where are those you have turned your back on? Where are those who have died? Where are the humans you have loved to ground your thought? To bring you back to earth? You are floating with planets and animals and various forms of light. You are floating in water, in air, in the quotidian nature of your thought, in the virtues and pieties you claim to flout. You are floating far out in the middle of a lake, under a billion bright stars, as in a sensory deprivation tank, drifting to the far reaches where no one can save you and your cries bounce off the trees like the call of a lonely coyote or cricket. No different than the way you walk through the autumn woods at dusk, a thousand so-called poems dying on the edge of your mumbling lips, those cold lips that have no time for kissing or speaking a soothing word. With blood in your boots, you stumble through the forest into trees as darkness gathers around you, becomes thick on the air, something you can almost taste. You have gone too far in the dwindling light and now are lost. Too proud to ask directions, too ingrained in your habits to stop mouthing words and to reach out and speak, to ask for help. All this mouthing of holy platitudes, all this mumbling of an inaudible prayer. Oh, autumn patriarch, how you have stumbled through the wet leaves and are blind.

III. The Light

An owl sounds in a far-off oak, calling to its mate after a night of silent hunting. Down in the ravine, a rustling of foxes, and not long after a panic of hares. The neighbors are safe in their accustomed beds. Why are we here? Why do we walk so far abroad? What other spirits of the night to share this damp and heady atmosphere? These formulations toss and turn like a shadow, fever dreams of far-flung constellations and pearls in opalescent galaxies, fever dreams, pertaining to fire, to heat. All is tense coiled nerve. A moth flutters in the streetlight, casting enormous shadows into the surrounding trees. Yet all is contained—no restless wind to carry our thoughts beyond these present dislocations. The light is disjointed and out of array, resting heavy on these sleepless lids, struggling to find purchase, among the jagged crags, on the face of the moon, the sidewalk, the canyon in its glory, the flash of the shutter. A little more light falls in, a little less falls out. Here is something lying face down. Here is something wan and ghostly.

Nadir Nahdi Lines Himself up with a Picture of His Indonesian Grandmother and They Look Alike

if not us, then maybe our faces will find a way home
                              maybe everything i needed to know

has always been corporeal
                              relied on the crinkle of eye

the beige of my mother and aunties
          who could only pass down certain pains for promised purity [?]

the brown of my father and uncles whom i have and will never meet
                              how smoke escapes our lips

at least i won't die after this
                              my heirlooms not gold but

think too much without forming lines across the forehead
                              have a gap between its teeth

my name won't matter one day
                    the last name will disappear to anecdote

indonesian will still finds its way out of my mouth like smoke
                    but i'll always know the shape of its lips

Winter Raiment

With winter's coming, almost anything may be
    sewn into a garment:

inside the hem tuck a tuft of shorn grass,
    yellowed now, but always scent of hay-summer,

within pockets, place a letter never sent, a photograph
    of someone unknown but loved, one small dried white bean,

at the bodice, select scarlet-beaded lobelia,
    not foxglove for therein lies no antidote.

Before turning and closing lapels, choose smooth flat river stones,
    allay worry before it comes,

and for the collar, hand stitch lavender bundles, picked as dew dries,
    such fragrance soothes a body's chills and fever.

It has been said if when sewing a coat, a drop of blood leaves stains,
    good fortune comes to the wearer,

Yet if this be not so, when you are gone, I wish to lay out garments
    to see your body's shape,

place my arms inside yours, and breast to chest to start your heart,
    and stop your leaving, slip into your skin.

Dear One, we have been forced to fashion cloth,
    cover ourselves from fresh and worn renderings,

learn between this winter and the next, there lies no protection, or
word,
    no stitches small or season-patterned enough to wear another—

    we just have to go uncloaked.

Heroism

It's late morning. A day in August. There are only a few people in the city park as I ride through it on the bike path. I ride this path every day when home from college. A slow moving creek in a man-made culvert lined with concrete flows alongside one side of the path. There are signs along the culvert that say, "No Swimming."

I can't swim.

In this heat the noise made by the cicadas that fill the oak and maple trees lining the path is almost deafening. In the meadow on the other side of the path, a boy about the age of thirteen is tossing a bright yellow Frisbee to his black and white border collie. I've seen them in the park before. I stop my bike at the edge of the path and take a drink from a water fountain standing a few feet from the culvert. My mother told me that when she was a little girl there were separate fountains for white and black people. The water from the fountain is tepid.

I lay my bike on its side in the grass and sit on the edge of the culvert. I can hear behind me the boy calling out, "Here, girl," to the dog.

A little girl suddenly appears at the edge of the culvert a few yards from me. She has blonde, curly hair. She stares at me for a few moments.

"I found a turtle here," she says. "My mom wouldn't let me take it home."

"That was probably best for the turtle," I say.

She holds up a hand, looks at it, than looks at me. "Your skin color is different than mine," she says.

I nod my head. "Yes, it is."

She comes closer. "How old are you?" she asks.

"Nineteen. How old are you?"

"Six," she says.

"Where's your mother?" I ask.

She points to the direction of where the boy is tossing the Frisbee to his dog. I turn to look around, searching for her parent, seeing only the boy and the border collie. In that instant I hear a splash in the water. I quickly turn and see the girl has fallen into the water. She's frantically splashing but not crying out. Without thinking, I jump into the water, grab onto her, and toss her onto the grass. Fighting the pull of the current I climb out of the culvert. The girl isn't breathing. I turn her on her side and thump on her back. She coughs and spits out water. I turn her onto her back and make sure she is breathing properly, and then pick her up and hold her in my arms.

Her mother comes running from a grove of oak trees. There is rage and fear in her eyes. "What are you doing to my little girl?" she screams at me. She slaps me, grabs the little girl, and runs off.

You

The bullet does not know malice. It does not understand hatred or
   revenge.
It only knows the material. What it does and, more importantly, does
   not touch.
It does not cry or laugh. It does not question or contemplate.

It plays God. It plays Satan. It plays you.

Life Among the Magnolias

The Mississippi River floods my blood.
 The muddy waters on my tongue.
  I was born in a town called   Death, Yazoo
 prophesized its own undoing.
 swallowed up
   by an infestation of leaves
    and left marooned in a sea of green.
 The corrupted stumps look like
 lonely beasts still lumbering to their Kudzu coffins.
   As if the thickets were deployed
   To consume the remains of all our wickedness
    scourged onto the land.
   See, Mississippi ain't all
   Lima beans and tire swings.
 Nah, there's sin stirred up in the mud
     Turning it to devil's clay.
      Mississippi was the foster parent
      That wrought the blues
       into creation.
   Those indigo hues
    cracked   from the syrinx of broken black birds.
   But malice was the lay of the land,
   and not just down in Dixie.
    See,
   I've learned
 to appreciate the stained kudzu blossoms
   that still ruminate on what was.
 Like them, I wrestle with the past and try to pin him down
   but I seek no absolution.

The Mississ,
         She ain't perfect
     But she sings to me –
   rolling pastures to amuse
and forests to sustain
the hot and sticky nights
in the back of beat up Jeeps,
     with the windows down,   us muttering
                               forbidden words
                                    soft and sweet.

                               No matter how I tried,
                               Never could outrun
                               where it is I'm from:

        this gold magnolia of a Deep South bloom.

Too Many Questions

Everyone says, "You'll appreciate
your mother when you have children."
I didn't. I needed to prove
she wouldn't understand or have the answers.
So many secrets, stories, unshared.

I conjure images of the two us
in the backseat of our family car,
my head in her lap. Me in bed beside her,
imitating the curl of her back, her hand
resting on her cheek as she slept.

I don't know when or why
I recoiled from her touch.
Why I spent years trying to separate,
ignoring her advances for closeness.
Annoyed if she called too often,
asked too many questions.

Her life, our life was ordinary.
(I won't be writing telltale memoirs or
revealing documentaries.)
I had no reason to push her away.

Now her mind grows blank, dark.
Too late for closeness, the kind I crave
from my own daughter,
which she freely gives me.
Although I don't always deserve it.

My mother doesn't call now, doesn't know
my number, remember it's my birthday
or hers. Doesn't know what to do
with her tea bag. Doesn't cook, sew.
She doesn't ask too many questions,
Just one over and over again; though it's
different each time I see her.

A damp, crumpled tissue holds a place
in my journal where I wrote this. I don't recall
leaving it there. But it's saturated,
with unspoken words, too many regrets.

KATHRYNN AXTON-ROOSEVELT

Mother Said There's a No-Smoking Section in Hell

yellow caution tape
thirty-seven seconds too late
one sip of beer
floating in acid
a steel table creaks
but never cries
peeling back our tongues
sealing them in a mostly empty
Folgers can
fragments of skull
dance effervescently
from pool of blood
to damp concrete
carelessly we flick our promises like
fingers yellowed and hollowed out
from the ends of stale cigarettes
looking on
we mourned
having never consumed
an authentic s'mores
we took another drag
falling through the pavement
like all the other remnants
of brother's beating heart.

Friend of Midnight

Moon, light—
witness to it:
apology

the bare tree
limbs
clasp like
fingers, trawling
the night for
for what you've
already known; and

for the first time,
you tell yourself
something you
usually reserve
for the comfort
of others.

Reflection on Love as Tinder Box

  i think i was lied to / when i was told love is abstract / terrified
that it was something you had to search for / in the dark of a dorm
room / with a deadbolt on the door / or in the flickering light in the
hallway of an apartment building / in north end / while you sit on the
stairs / a stranger / putting a hand on your shoulder / inviting you to
warm up inside / or / that it was commodity / something to barter /
to exchange / what do i have to give of myself that comes with any
hesitation? / what is a sincere offering that i would not embrace with
tenderness?/ yes / i know that i was lied to / love is free and here /
and i've seen the shape of love / bigger than my body / perhaps that is
what scared me about the way love was always presented / as if i only
had five feet and five inches to contain it / making the hearth of me
too small and too finite / for everyone i love to warm themselves by
/ or worse / that i can only be loved as a hearth / as a thing to kneel
in front of / to use / until the blood is thawed and moving / and my
kindles are put out / i think i am afraid of someone / mistaking my
glow through the window for an act of arson / maybe that's why i
always drew the curtains in / in time / i will learn to light myself /
and leave the doors unlocked / and / isn't that the shape of love / an
unlocked door / the trust that someone will walk in and allow you to
be warm with them / without the expectation of burning / without
the overfeeding of tinder / and the projections of shadows on the
walls / tonight / i am sitting with them / each flicker of my heart a
pause of speech / and in the lucent glow / i see the details of their face
/ smiling and laughing / and i am concrete and tangible / not girl as
hearth / not as metaphor / not as abstraction /

yes / love is free and it is here /

The White Speck Dancing by the Window

reminds of snow when life was lived there.
those cold winds forcing the collar tight

the bears in the lightly dusted boreal
preparing the last of their supplies before
the ground freezes over until spring

children begging the sky for a storm
to crown the water tower hill for sledding
ahead of mothers calling them home

the romantic, for a white Christmas.
the young woman, to blanket herself
with her lover by an open flame.

for crisp star-filled nights where the only
clouds are of spoken words whispered
in the knowledge of being heard. yes. yes.

I miss the north on days like these.
I miss home.

The Noise

I sit awake hearing the sounds.
Listening, wondering if I will sacrifice myself to
whatever is making that noise. I slowly and quietly
grab my bat, tiptoe down the hall.
I shout a sound—I stepped on something.
I keep walking, not allowing myself to
turn on the light to see whatever
noise it is. I keep going. It's getting louder
as if the sound is on top of me!
Soon as I stop, the noise stops.
As I go forward, the noise does too.
Finally I realize
I am making the noise and
I feel like such a dummy
and I laugh.

Love Story

Every day the boy walked to the wall. He brought a ladder, a trowel, mortar, and a few bricks with him. He inspected it carefully, sealing cracks, replacing bricks as needed. He maintained the wall diligently, as the monster clicked and chattered behind it. His family didn't know the monster was there. They didn't know where he went every day when he was taking care of the wall. He knew, in the intuitive way that children do, that if he told his family about the monster, it would destroy them. He, a child, carried this burden alone, in silence, to protect his family. He cared for the wall for many years. One day, when he was almost a man, he met a girl, who was almost a woman. She told him about her monster. How she told her family about it and it destroyed them. He didn't tell her about his wall, or his monster. She felt she could be honest with him, to tell him things she never told anyone else. Maybe she knew in some intuitive way that he understood. They loved each other. Still, he kept the wall and his monster a secret. Many years passed. One day, when the woman was very sad thinking about her monster, the man said he had something to show her. He took her hand and led her to the wall. He picked up his trowel and carefully chipped away the mortar around a single brick. He pulled the brick out and said "Look." She peered inside, and to her surprise, she saw a monster there, chittering and slithering around, unaware it was being watched. It had hands, with big knuckles and long, clubbed fingers that grabbed at and touched what didn't belong to it. It had a mouth, slick with saliva, that whispered lies. It had eyes, bulging and unblinking, that sought out innocence and vulnerability. The woman was stunned. The man had kept this from her, from everyone, for so long. She couldn't look away as it crept and slid around. Something got its attention and its head turned the other way. She saw it had a second face. She had known this face for years. She had invited it into her home, spent holidays with it, consoled it at wakes and memorial services. The woman was enraged. She began tearing at the opening in the wall, knocking pieces of mortar away and ripping bricks out. She wanted vengeance. She wanted to tear the head off the monster and show everyone its two faces. To drag his family into the blinding light of reality to see that the face they knew was a lie and what lay behind it was a monster.

As she tore a hole through the wall she heard the man speak softly behind her. "Please don't tell." And when she turned, he was the boy he used to be. And she was the girl she used to be. They fixed the wall together until everything was as it had been. They walked away hand-in-hand, the secret now carried between them.

LindaAnn LoSciavo

When Fathers Disappear

When fathers disappear, they take their name—
Along with the certainty they loved those who
Were left behind, deserted. Families
Can overwinter, silent, wondering.

Perhaps his name was fake, an alias.

Deceptive Dad erase all memories:
Cold righteous looks, prophetic sighs, door slams.
He'd been a mouthpiece, a provider once.
Imaginative words, incisive wit
Will introduce himself to women's eyes,
Who'll see potential, dream's aristocrat,
Misreading his moods for profundity.

All unaware, one blindly takes him in.

Compliance has its price, which makes him twitch,
Then adumbrate new plans each time he shaves.
When gearshifts of a train have more appeal
Than bottomless parental collar-grabs,
He'll leave for cigarettes and not return—
Nor face those bad names touching everything.

Birth of a Navy Vet

You see stars when loosening bolts
that were gronked too tight.
A drunk bubblegummer, deployed
somewhere beyond the clouds,
gronking bolts over the desert.
Oily grin shines
in the darkness of crawl spaces,
not considering those
who'll come later, humming
a tune, gronking bolts.
Gronking them star-tight.

Sad

If I don't look,
I won't see,
those dirty ass men
looking at me
throw the bottle back,
squint my eyes
Where the hell did
my life fucking go.

My eyes is hollow my
wrists are scarred.

I'm thinking, I'm
thinking, Why am I in
the back of this car,
empty beer bottles
scattered at my feet,
the scent of Man
lingering in the seats.

That Summer Night Holding Long

Bushmaster said "You hear that? The talking blues, those are the ancestors you hear. They remember. You can't erase the past, you can't burn it away. That's the spell on you, that's magic. Science in its purest form." And I replied yes, shamefully it took me 18 years and Gisela's persistence to visit 18th and Vine, but that's what happens when you grow up in a place where your parents teach you the off tempo rhythm of locking your doors at red lights downtown instead of them making you listen to the blues that billow out of Gates BBQ smokestacks, and Gisela made us read every placard and put on every set of headphones at the American Jazz Museum so we could hear Billie Holiday take lyrics written by a Jewish man who devoured every word of ancestors that weren't his, 2 years before he would see his own European family forced into ghettos, and turn it into the song of the century like only a black woman could do after seeing her father die outside of a hospital where a sign hung that said "Whites Only," pouring every ounce of agony into a brittle microphone until it shattered, leaving her handcuffed to a hospital bed where a new kind of hatred poured out of her liver.

Leaving Massachusetts

Before the maple leaves have a chance
to set themselves on fire again, and
summer has ticked off its annual checklist:
        Day lilies—done.
        Irises—done.
        Hedge roses, lavender, blackberries—done.
That's when I haul the suitcases down from the attic.
Check the date on my passport. Pull up weather reports
to see what's falling from foreign skies.

The cat will miss you, my brother says.
But I know what he means.
We who have six decades behind us
don't need to belabor good-byes. He
was always the rooted part
of our family tree, and I
the wind-borne seed.

Leaving Massachusetts has been habit-forming,
its airport knows me well enough
to leave the key under the doormat.
I grow weary of the weather's mood swings,
from the scolding tongue of February
to September's sycophantic praise.
The backhanded slap of its summer sun
has reddened my cheek more than once.
I say I won't return, but something
always turns me around.

What is it about this bay state
that raises its scrawny arm to beckon me
homeward? Every town, every highway sign,
every peak and pillar, is saturated
with something remembered—
the first time I sang, or walked, or loved,
or grieved, or bore a child,
my first of every everything
was always here.

Rebirth

The photograph shows two little boys, arms encircling each other, smiling innocently into the camera. The boys' cherubic features, once sharp and clear, are now muted by a reddish tinge as if the entire photograph's been dipped in red wine. Maggie snorts with frustration as she moves the photograph closer, peering intently, desperately trying to wish the image into clarity. Every photograph in the album has the same reddish hue. The cherished memories of her boys fading into oblivion. The gentle tapping of a branch against the window catches her attention, she smiles, then whispers, "I'm coming."

Turning the pages of the album, Maggie contemplates the baby pictures pressed beneath the aging plastic sleeve. The newborns, legs curled up, arms akimbo, reminding her of two plucked chickens. As she fumbles with the album, Maggie attempts to squeeze the photograph out from under the plastic's vise-like grip. Probing between the photograph and the plastic she chides herself with, "A few dollars saved. Why on earth did I buy such cheap film? I should have bought the Kodak." But Maggie already knows the answer to her question. Cheap film meant money saved and money saved meant special treats for the boys, especially their favorite, Apple Whizz Fizz.

Laughing to herself, she recalls the boys jumping up and down in front of her and squealing with excitement as they tried to guess which hand held the Apple Whizz Fizz.

"Which hand?"

"That one, Mummy?"

"You sure?"

"Yes, that one, that one."

Such wonderful days filled with giggles and laughter and Apple Whizz Fizz coated teeth.

Her boys spilling Whizz Fizz on the kitchen floor and her pretending to be angry. Maggie tasting the Whizz Fizz and being surprised by the sudden tingling burst of flavor on her tongue. Such wonderful days when she made them happy with just a packet of Apple Whizz Fizz.

At last the picture is free. Pressing the image to her lips, Maggie bestows a kiss, a gentle benediction on the two babies. With closed eyes she recalls the pulling sensation as her breast let down her milk for their suckling, their eyes staring up at her, taking in her every nuanced expression. Her fingers long to touch the soft down of their hair.

The staccato rhythm of the branch against the window pane breaks her reverie. She slips the photograph back into its sacred place amongst the other beloved photographs and turns to the last page in the album. This page holds a newspaper cutting yellowed with age.

"FRIENDS' PRANK TURNS TO TRAGEDY:

An April Fools' Day prank by a group of friends turned to tragedy when a boy drowned trying to save his twin brother at Scarborough Beach. Both boys died in the incident."

Closing the album, Maggie walks outside into the back garden and smiles lovingly at the two huge apple trees standing sentinel on either side of her window. Each tree's branches reach out, embracing the other, creating a sanctuary of shade and sweet perfume. One branch scrapes against the window, making a tapping noise in the evening breeze. The trees are thirty years old, their trunks gnarled with age, but their branches heavy with the gift of apple blossom.

Maggie pats the nearest tree's trunk, her aged skin rubbing against the dry nodules of bark. Lowering her body, her fingers digging into the fragrant earth as she touches the exposed root system, Maggie leans gently against the trunk. She recalls the night she dug the two holes, the grief still alive and jagged in her chest. Placing a snippet of their cherished baby hair in the pungent earth of each hole, Mikey on the left and Marty on the right. Covering each son's hair with a sapling apple tree bursting with life. For thirty years she watched the saplings grow into these mighty apple trees towering above her, apple trees that can live for one hundred years.

As the evening breeze whispers its promises of the night, Maggie leans against the trunk of her beloved tree and softly hums to herself the ancient pagan chant of rebirth and hope, "All that dies shall be reborn."

Lunatic

The madness dims
After months of it.
Like lemon, like milk
Your name fades
Where it is written
On each of my ribs.
The filaments of your fingers
Bear no tenor of sun. They cannot
Move through me like radiation.
Your voice no longer medication.
Your mouth is no key to the jacket
That has held me straight.
My hands are free
My mind is not what it was
But it is mine
And I will walk from this place,
A free woman.

North Sentient Island Tribe

A man from Mumbai died
due to old age organ failure.
He was disgusted with the life
in so-called civilized society.
"What civilization is this?"
he wondered and left his body.
Science has brought pollution
that has engendered dreaded diseases
like cancer, heart ailments, what not?
He found when dresses are discovered
to cover private parts, it is violated
by semi-nude dresses that make
the hungry eyes more thirsty.
This ultimately ends up to rape
that is the worst product of civilized
modern people on this ill-fated earth.

North sentient island in Andaman
has an aboriginal tribe living in isolation
for about sixty thousand years.
They all, young and old, are mostly nude.
The man from Mumbai took birth there.
He remembered his previous birth
and was astounded how this tribal community
is spiritually more elevated than
civilized people of modern world.
Their women are naked but
that does not cause birth of illegitimate
offspring inundating shelters of orphans.
Their number also is not bursting like
virus and bacteria causing threat of longevity
of the poor earth they are inhabiting.
He again wondered, "Who is more civilized?"

Tongue, Swallowed

after Ouyang Jianghe

What a thing it would be, if we all could fly.
Still flight is but a word caught at the junction

of dirt & sky, tail hooking like a lure.
In a dream I saw myself loose-palmed & hollow

a ring of birds sitting gagged at my feet,
empty cistern begging to be choked.

This was the story you told me:
a pair of swallows circling over forest fire,

muscle & fringe turning ash/gale/limbo.
Springtime and you taught me

what it meant to be free—
a body of dough battered by the wind,

silent howl through the air.
Asphyxiation stuck throat-deep

& a tongue, limp and motherless
—remember, you are nothing

but a word. So picture this:
in Chinese, the word for swallow

is made up of a wide, heaving
mouth, a pair of wings unfurled.

& before I wake, the dream will end with
my voice crackling to a warble that repeats

my name like an anthem.

Down This River

Through the crumbling
corridors of time
filled with distant echoes,
down this voiceless river
my rowboat's still drifting.

Does darkness or light
awaits me with the next ripple,
yet to be born?

My dreams,
washed out at shore
wave back at me
and slowly sink
into the twilight haze.

If I could stop
and hold them, feel them,
run them
through my aging fingers
for a breath or two.

But time doesn't stop,
this river never stops,
it never stops, this rowboat
that's taking me away
from what has happened
and what has not.

Ripple by ripple
I'm getting closer
to where I came from—
the Mother Sea
that gave a birth
to this silent river
some thousands or so
ripples ago.

The Tired World

I want to get under a blanket
to hide myself from winter's cold
and lie... My soul is so tired
of cleaning up this tired, tired house.

Of entertaining this tired, angry world,
the world of tired strangers
who are not the right ones
and don't care about my afflictions...

I touch the tired mirror.
The patina is weary of long, tiring years...
Where are the right ones, what road do they plod along?
Or probably they don't exist at all in this tired world?

Nobody cares of your fatigue.
Everyone is brimful of their own.
Happiness is actually a mere trifle:
a bit of summer again, just half an hour of summer...

To lie down on the sand
and listen to the crashing waves
and understand: there is no death.
There is only a promise of peace,
of a break from the stupefying years.

From the useless meetings, revelations,
from my stupid errors and losses.
From my own fatigue and laziness.
Or probably I am also not the right one?

Our tired hearts collapse,
unable to stand the separation and waiting.
So take care of your soul and soothe it to calm.
It's going to soothe you till the very end...

DIANE MASUCCI

Alice's Restaurant

Alice stared at her bird feeder, filled with suet and seed, wondering if the baby chicadees and cardinals, so vibrant against the snow, would access her offerings.

Two squirrels, brown and vigorous, waited on the maple tree branch, swishing their tails to and fro, eyeing her feeder. Damn it, she whispered to herself as she pawed through her grey metal recipe box for a dinner plan. Why can't I find an anti-squirrel feeder, one that might even, she thought darkly, electrocute the wicked wiry long-tailed rats?

Under "S" in her recipe box was an ancestor's final solution for those critters: Squirrel soup.

If she were back home in Louisiana she might have pulled out her granddaddy's rifle and knocked those buggers right out of the tree. No, no, no, another voice told her, you don't live there anymore, Alice Faye girl. You're up north now in a sedate colonial town with picket fences and neighbors who can see and hear what you are doing. She still had a gun but no permit in this New Jersey town where the only gunslingers were the local police.

It was unlikely that any emergency squad or firefighters would come to her poor feathered friends' rescue. They only rescue cats.

Neighbors often asked where she was from on account of her accent.

She chose a chicken casserole for dinner and would make a fruit salad for a side.

Her eyes landed on the wooden broom standing tall and handy at the back door. No, not tall enough for that. But as she watched the squirrels begin their trek across the branches, she remembered a better weapon.

Her son had last year carved a slingshot out of wood; where was it? Alice climbed the stairs to her son's room, hoping she might preserve the birds' feast. Her hands found the splendid weapon on the top shelf of the closet.

Now, she vowed, they had a chance.

Pedigree

time would have you believe that she creeps slowly
though a crane-necked woman knows otherwise
my mind duplicitous and narrow
shrieks out wordlessly
for I am nothing more
than mother's most precious ghost story
father reminded that
dogs and Indians are counted
in quantum leaps
"and how lucky my girl
you get to be both
yet neither"
this body is eternal winter
my spirit, once a warrior on fire
now a brittle bear hoping
each warm breath in hibernation
a temptation for death's frigid hands
I am four conflicting pieces of furniture
or a poem failed
collaboratively
I told my grandmother once
that I was Cottonwood
"ugly trees grow beautiful flowers"
she said—
leading me to believe that
there's something to be said for age and wisdom
not much,
but something

Prayer Whistle Them into Song Air

Michael wasn't born religious
but he found Jesus
in the moshpit
of a christian
hardcore show.
He came from a place
of privilege
that allowed him to choose
instead of grasp onto God
as a last resort, a hope that
somewhere beyond the physical
world, there is freedom.
So when he scoffed loudly
and stormed away from Chance
the Rapper's gospel, I let him go
because the show wasn't for him,
it wasn't even for me.
Cynthia Marie Graham Hurd
Susie Jackson
Ethel Lee
Lance Depayne Middleton-Doctor
Clementa C. Pinckney
Tywanza Sanders
Daniel Simmons
Sharonda Coleman-Singleton
Myra Thompson
Names worth etching into an echo
like "Don't
believe in kings, believe in the kingdom."
like
"When the praises go up,
the blessings go down."

The Indifferent

Jasmine scowls at the back of the man's head. Ignorant heads seem more irritating when they're viewed from behind. She thinks she could just tear the headphones off his head and hurl them through the cabin space.

Instead, Jasmine inhales deeply and turns back to the window. The sunset is still in full yellow and orange glory, stretching infinite, aching her heart. The light illuminates the bending, curving river below, which rests on the land like a gigantic dormant serpent.

Africa.

Jasmine quickly discovers that, like Headphones Guy, the locals are also indifferent toward and unmoved by the natural wonders around them. They carry on with their lives, hustling about, chatting on their phones, even as mighty Mount Kilimanjaro stands in their midst like the abode of something even more pure and heavenly than the mountain itself. The only locals who go up there, or to the other places of natural wonders, are those who have to go: safari guides, porters and lodge staff. Kilimanjaro, Ngorongoro Crater, Tarangire, and the Serengeti National Parks are mere jobsites to them, workplaces they are obligated to turn up at.

Jasmine would do their jobs for free, and happily so. Or at least so she believes, but then unwittingly her camera comes out, and she starts snapping away at every entity of aforementioned wonder she encounters: the elongated giraffe necks, the enormity of hippopotamuses and elephants, the litheness of the impala, the numerous zebra stripes, the proud, striding ostriches. Jasmine spares no thought that these animals formed after millions of years of savage evolution, for the sake of sheer survival and not for pudgy office folk to ooh and aah at; office workers who only requested photos because they didn't think of anything better to say when Jasmine said that she was going to Africa for her vacation. She understands all this, however, only at the airport, waiting to depart from Africa. By then, of course, it's too late.

It's ultimately too late when, in a half-dozing haze, she hears the pilot say—in a worried tone—something about engine failure. Screams and sobbing fill the airplane, which is now in an unstoppable fall toward inevitable impact. Pieces of the craft are torn away with the wind as it plummets. Passengers soon follow. Headphones Guy is torn from his seat before Jasmine is. Beyond fear and in a state of quiet that might just be shock, Jasmine thinks, well, at least those headphones are finally ripped from his head. Screams and cries can still be heard all around her as people are whipped about and tossed around by the winds.

Suddenly, she thinks, everyone's so aware of the Earth now, that Earth that will receive and incorporate their corpses into itself, with the same indifference that they had beheld it.

Talking to My Family About Emily Dickinson

"Yo bro," my brother texted me,
  Who was that woman whose house we saw in Amherst?
  She won competitions baking bread,
  Her father was some kind of bigshot?"
  I provide him with a name. Years later my mother:
"I went to a film in the old age home,
  this woman. American. They were so religious.
  She never married. Her sister didn't.
  They drove off her brother because he fooled around
  With this woman. He was already hitched.
  They kept reading out her poems. I didn't think they were all that.
  But what an existence. Do you know what they call that?
  This disease, just trembling like a leaf?"
  I say I don't know the name
  Then hang up and say my prayers.
  My father would have known a bit
  About her lines that were hand stitched
  Into tiny little books she left
  And sent occasionally to relatives.
  But he died in his own armchair, saying my mother's pet name
  And most of what he wrote is now in files
  Waiting to be cleared when she no longer knows he's dead.
  Emily Dickinson's sister-in-law saw to it she was framed
  In a tapestry bigger than Amherst, each line a window pane
  For some meadow she never claimed,
  But when they call and ask me
  Who she was, what was her name?
  I say she baked bread and you can taste the crust
  Even though she never sold a crumb or left a recipe you could pass
    down.

The Never Ones

Mom and Grandma would whisper, using German as their secret adult language. Like many second-generation Americans, I couldn't speak my family's first language, but I understood some of it—that *scham* meant shame, that *schwanger* meant pregnant. At age thirteen, I overheard that my mother suffered a miscarriage at age fifteen. I wondered how she'd felt, how her parents reacted. I even felt disappointed. It meant I wasn't her first. I wasn't jealous, though. How can you resent someone whose brief existence lay in shadow?

After knowing about Mom's teen pregnancy, I could be more patient with Grandma later, as she pulled me away from beer-besotted men at Octoberfest and interrogated my dates.

I adored Grandma, but never knew Mom's dad. Grandma and Grandpa divorced in Germany, years before I was born. Mom would only say, "We've lost touch," with a pursing of the lips that signaled an end to the topic. I learned to quit asking, just as I sensed not to tell anyone that I knew about the miscarriage.

I always wanted to link the two, Grandpa and the baby, the never born and the never seen—hiking the Black Forest, kicking a soccer ball—imagined Grandpa returned, our kitchen full of forgiveness.

Mom finally told me, years later, two months before they both slipped out of her consciousness forever. The baby would have been both my brother and uncle.

She sobbed, spoke of limbs tangled, something about the eyes, a blessing and twisted, and oh, how she bled.

Paying Guest

Last time I saw her
as a teenage girl.
Long ago I used to
visit them at week end
after my office work,
enjoyed being together
as her mother liked
me as a brother.
I did not have any relative
at that place far away
from the city of my birth.
I left my mother
at a young age.
I missed her miserably,
lonely lamenting
longing for her love
like a lotus for a lake.
Landed lastly
as a paying guest
on her mother's insistence.

Three long decades passed.
"Where were you?"
Neither you nor I
had any contact at all.
Time rolled over my life
I became an old man,
about to retire,
exhausted in working life,
preparing to go back
to my native place
just as a soldier returns
home after war.

STEPHEN O'DONNELL

Cut

My father did not want me to be cut. He had wanted me to
be a whole woman. With my mother's silence and grandmother's
collaboration, I was mutilated. They had been cut themselves. They
were of a different time, an older way. They did not want me to die
alone and unloved. As though a small piece of my own flesh would
deter a husband.

They do not know night or day, only the constant firelight of the
hut. They lie on woven reeds atop a dirt floor. Theirs is a world of
scent. The sweet must of their mothers' breasts. Woodsmoke. The
walls of hard dried dung. They have never felt the wind at dusk nor
smelled the rains. One morning the child awakes. The air is different.
She breathes without the concurrent breath alongside her own. Her
cousin is gone. Her mother too is gone, replaced by a old woman,
lean armed. Smelling of moss. The cool underbrush.

She has come to cut away a piece of womanhood. For
womanhood. In the name of the harvest. By moonlight the old
woman carries the small nub of flesh down to the riverbank and
casts it into the muddied waters. To be carried forgotten to sea. To be
swallowed whole by sturgeon. Crocodiles watch her with prehistoric,
unwearied eyes.

Now I am old. My husband's long dead. My children are gone far
from me in miles and in time. Just as I am distant from the lands of
my mothers.

In Response to the Intellectual's Groundbreaking Thesis that Race Is a Social Construct

And of course
I am aware of the biblical advice
not to build one's house
upon sand.
I imagine that sand had a past somewhere
way back when
it was more than the butt end
of a parable.
But what, I ask you,
is sand except the remains
of rocks rubbing each other
the wrong way?
And who am I,
but another body rubbed raw,
washed upon a shore full
of beach houses
constructed from palm tree bark
held together by wet
then sunbaked sand bricks?
What you call an imaginary
shelter, I call a childhood.
My house is about as constructed
as time, and according to my watch,
another hurricane is on the horizon.
And my view of the sun—
an arm's length away from
an ocean that can't decide
between swallowing me whole and
spitting my bones
onto the shore or
dragging my body out
further with each tide
to never be seen again—
looks a helluva lot better from
my bedroom window.

JAMIE SAMDAHL

How I Will Explain the Rape to My Daughter

Muddled like mint at the bottom of a glass   lit up with pain
brighter than halogen   premonitions of shame
the jade bracelet cracked against the wall   my voice
retracted hard as a peach pit & lodged behind my navel
my brother passed out nearby   sleeping
through it all   violence wearing the prettiest
porcelain mask   the room painted some safe color
then the worst of it   unlearning my love for him

The Kiss

In twenty-five years she'd kissed 523 dying men—old ones and young ones, lawyers and janitors, teachers and architects. And Amy had never once been caught, not until today. Her husband didn't know. Tad thought she tossed in bed at night because of the life and death nature of her job. As a teacher, the worst part of his day was breaking up a fistfight or handling a disgruntled parent.

Sometimes he would find her staring at the half moon at 2 a.m. He'd wrap his arms around her small shoulders and plant a kiss on her neck.

This Monday, though, when Amy's lips had just touched the clammy face of John Berry, a voice blurted out, "Why are you kissing that patient?"

Amy turned around to discover Dr. Goldstein in the room. She looked at the patient and saw a pale pink mark on his gray lips. So finally I'm caught, she thought, letting out a sigh. She turned back to face her accuser. His bald head seemed sweaty and his green eyes seemed small and narrow. Though he was five foot nine inches, today he seemed like a giant in this shrinking room.

"He's going to die," she said simply.

She spoke so softly that Dr. Goldstein moved closer to hear her.

"He's going to die. Alone. I just wanted to...."

How could she make him understand? Dr. Goldstein had four children and a wife. He wouldn't die alone.

"You can't do this. This. No." He shook his head and wiped his brow. A loud voice blared from the intercom and his beeper vibrated.

"We'll talk later. Don't do this again." His voice trailed off as he left in a hurry.

Amy reviewed the rules again, trying to rationalize her behavior. As she ticked away the numbers with fingers, her hands trembled. One, men only. Two, dying men. Three, no spouse, no significant other. Four, men who will die alone.

Every night she still pictured that first patient, Derrick Ryan. Amy had been a new twenty-four-year-old ER nurse, just returned from her honeymoon. He'd been brought in with too many injuries. Motorcycle crash. Blood everywhere. Thick eyebrows and blue eyes, pale as the summer sky.

"Kiss me," Derrick Ryan, age twenty-one, had whispered.

But she had not kissed him. Regret kept her company at night. Would it have been so terrible if she had granted this final request?

So, she'd kissed dying men. Trying for twenty years to relieve the guilt of not granting a man his last kiss. And now she'd been caught. I don't care if they fire me, she thought. She reached out and touched Mr. Berry's hand. It was growing cold. He would be gone by tomorrow.

Out in the hallway, she heard quiet sobbing. A nurse pushed a cart, and a candy striper smiled. As her white shoes quietly moved forward, she closed her eyes. Amy felt 523 kisses all over her face, one by one lifting her through the halls of the hospital.

Sounds I Can't Hear

If you were to ask me
what are the sounds I can't hear,
I would sit here and think, in awe,
how does one NOT hear and feel every single moment in time,
every ping of the pen, every pang of the pain,
every heartbeat in China, every gunshot in Spain?
I hear your pulse, I feel your love, I see your smile,
I hear your lies.
I hear the baby crying for her momma.
I hear every tree as it falls.
I wish it were only my ears I can hear with.

Jukebox

Glamour in a little blue bottle
April in Paris

Imagine yourself
Marilyn in Monroe
in black face,
Pancake makeup
a daily disappointment

Burgundy lips,
round hips
poured into red polyester

three-inch heels
Carry your sway and
buried regrets
Sam Cooke's rhythms shimmy down inside,
Soften
help
to mistake identities

Repetitious
next day's blues
Lost/found lovers
Ripped nylons
broken red nail polish
broken visions
reflections in a broken mirror
reflections in a $20 room

A New Lonely

being pregnant
then not
leaves no room for air
a life
then no life
causes the in-laws from Ohio
to say things like
"It wasn't meant to be"
and
"God works in mysterious ways"
it's hard to imagine God
having anything
to do with it
the sonogram tech stopped talking
and left the room
while looking at her shoes
as if
the heartbeat on the screen
two weeks before
was now hiding
in the soft insoles
of her worn leather clogs
the lives
those shoes
must carry
when a baby dies,
dreams get strange
and waking up alone is
a new kind of
loneliness

January 1986

Kate says if you put a buttercup under your chin, it lights up your face. I try it on Apollo, but he ends up eating it and licking my nose after. We run through the meadow trying to catch the sun, falling over and laughing, pretending we burned our hands. Apollo has a bad hip so he turns back when we reach the treehouse. He's not allowed in it anyway—girls only.

There are six steps up the trunk of the tree we painted the rainbow colors. We sit on stacks of books, telling our innermost secrets like letting out a light only we can see. I put my cassette in the boom box; it blasts Madonna and we dance until we are dizzy.

A big ball of fire expands and drops from the clouds. Our parents run to find us.

The television, which is almost never on, speaks about the teacher who fell from the sky. President Reagan addresses us, the light missing from his eyes.

Wrap Me In Vermont

On my way to Vermont
to a writers' camp
even though I'm not a writer

I saw him
But didn't want to
the man with the pretty smile
the "hi, pretty lady" talking man

the one who lives at the shelter

He's standing on the top stair
of the Atlantic Avenue
train stop

His brown hand showed
the lighter side
and he said

"Please, got a dollar,
a quarter,
a di…?"

When he saw me
"dime" got stuck in the air
like it was waiting
waiting for something else to push it out of the way

I looked at his face, his eye, his shadow
I forced a smile out, a
"How you doin, brother?"

But that day
he didn't
smile
didn't
flirt
didn't
charm

He turned, jammed his
hands into empty pockets
his rounded shoulders resting
in my eyes

his size couldn't conceal
his need
his new life
on the streets of Brooklyn

I swallowed my conscience
left him there
his head hung
my head hung
his lost smile stuck
in my chest
But I shoved my hands in my pockets
and went on to Vermont
To a writer's camp,
Even though I'm not a writer

For Coicou

Sorry, Coicou
Sorry, I said
I don't want New York to define
domestic Violence.

And I said Margarita and SuiLin didn't
need to hear about verbal abuse.
And that domestic violence to them
is different than domestic violence is
to me--to you.

Sorry I said nothing--did nothing.

Your bleeding bed,
unmade by your husband's
sharpened machete
left you in parts and pieces
to greet the morning sun,
and your children's morning romp.

Sorry I didn't know
that your half smile,
your oversized clothes,
your uncombed hair,
the need and urgency of your hello,
your hasty steps away from my door each week,
carried more than food pantry groceries.

Sorry I didn't ask
sorry I didn't tell
sorry to be sorry.

But sorry won't
put your pieces
back together again, Coicou.

Sorry won't give him another chance
to think it over, Coicou.
And sorry won't bring us back your missing smile
for a proper burial.

Quest in the Depth

In the ocean of thoughts
I search for you in vain
all narrowness swims shallow
as small fishes—
desire, money, sex galore.
I try to filter them out
to peep into the deep
with the hope to get a glance.
You are so pure
my dirty hand cannot touch.
At the peak of a moment of serenity
when a sacred feeling drenches me
and my love for you turns me into tears
I feel myself so empty that I lament
why I am so mean!
How I can reach you, my beloved!
Tears roll down the cheek
day dips into night,
oh my love you never come
I am unable to cross the depth.

Below the Remembering Mind

Generally I am not free to follow the light
Into the darker rooms
Where I live…in search…
To find the golden thread
Or the crystal ball
In the dream of the world
Where rules do not apply
And stoplights are never red.

Yesterday it appeared
That I should attempt to leave
This common world with names
On streets and old maps
Numbered houses
And seek a larger habitation

The silent night is a separate story
Maybe somewhere in childhood
The opportunity to see the whole
In the part, to take the catalogue
Of my presence, the whole story
And sort the pages, rearranging
The order to find missing parts

Like the history of a river
As a human experience
Discovering a nameless address
And the unseen, underwater terrain
Below the remembering mind

Sometime yesterday
The big yesterday that began
With my great-great grandparents
Our Old Man River, and all the
Tributaries now pushing for
Promise in the spring. The thaw
And the rush of fresh water
Once upon a time again

Among Jazzy's Effects

This old photograph, heirloom silver patina,
leached color like a skull exposed
to sun and sand scour,
one a drugstore cowboy
might lift from a gallery wall in, say Taos,
take to his New York apartment, display—
an objet d'art to
illustrate worldliness and taste,
western objects being in.
Yellowed, the photograph
perhaps hung in a smoking room,
breathed nicotine until saturated.
But, peer closely;
see a young man: severely-cut suit,
flattened hat upon his head—
boater it's called—
beside an older man, a brother or young uncle
more at ease, boater casually at his side.
The young woman, arrogant tilted chin,
cants her eyes
as though appraising both men,
demonstrates herself bound to neither.
Her skirts gather, likely not in a bustle,
since they'd passed from fashion,
but who can attest
to a young woman's whims?
She is perhaps Jazzy's great-grandmother
or great-grand aunt,
someone she met as a child,
repulsed by shrunken form, taloned grasp,
though here she remains a girl,
peach plump and rosy.

In this boardwalk scene, imagine
the trio strolls to a seaside restaurant,
orders oysters. She will season one
with a squeeze of lemon,
lift the shell to her lips. This is her world,
salty, more difficult to swallow
than she'd have guessed.

Be the Deer

For eight and a half minutes after the motorcycle accident, I slipped in and out of consciousness until the flashing lights of the paramedics shone across the wet pavement, and I let go and slipped under. What I remember most of those eight and a half minutes was the breath of the deer against my forehead and her rapid heartbeat under her breast, her heart racing with fear, but it felt like her heart was pounding so fast to keep mine going. I remember thinking, I could be dying on this country road, a quarter mile from my wife and kids, and the last soul I'll share my life with is this deer.

The deer had skittered into the road, and though I'd been driving my bike at 35 miles per hour, I didn't have a chance to brake before we collided, slid across the wet leaves together, and wound up pinned under a guardrail lining a ravine. The bulk of the deer stopped me from falling down the ravine and into the creek below.

So, in one sense, the deer saved my life.

When I woke up after five hours of surgery, I turned my head to feel for the deer. I wanted her warm breath, her strong heartbeat. "Where is—?" I asked.

"She's right here," a nurse said, and I felt the familiar hand of my wife against my forehead, breathed the scent of the calendula cream that she prepares in small batches. As comforted as I felt by her touch and familiar scent, I wondered what had happened to the deer. Had she survived? Surely her vitals had been strong, strong enough to encourage mine, but what happened after the paramedics separated us? I had seen a lot of blood, spilling across the pavement. Had it all been mine? Or was it hers too? The feeling I couldn't shake was that our breaths and heartbeats had merged in those eight and a half minutes and our lives were forever connected.

When the bright lights from the ambulance had shone, had she felt fear? I knew she had felt fear when we crashed—her adrenaline had mixed with mine and resounded through my body. In between the crash and the ambulance arriving, she had provided a serene calm. Her breath had eased from a mad snort to a steady in and out. When I remembered to breathe, I tried to match her rhythm. She had not only blocked me from falling down the ravine, but her calm breathing had also saved my life.

Looking at my legs, several days later, I saw bruising indicating that I'd been kicked by hooves. I didn't remember any kicking. Maybe when the paramedics had arrived, she'd struggled to free herself from our embrace.

When cornered, deer have a fierce kick. The only human killed by wildlife in Yosemite National Park was a tourist who harassed a deer long enough for hugs that he was kicked to death.

My deer had been alive, but I was the only one who wondered what happened to her. To the doctors, to my wife, she was someone to blame the accident on. To them, she was the trigger that sent me to the ER on a dark November evening when I should have been sitting down to one of my wife's roasts.

To me, we shared a spiritual bond equaling the moments I first held my children as babies. I remember singing to them and soothing them as their mother lay in bed, recovering. Now it is my turn to recover.

I comforted myself by thinking that once she saw I was safe, my deer slipped away into the woods, licked her minor wounds, and returned to her own family.

With her, she took a part of me. A part that will forever live in the Pennsylvania woods, carefully negotiating the country roads overrun with impatient drivers. When she drinks from a stream, when she grazes, when she nuzzles her young, a part of me will share these activities.

While a part of her stays with me, here in my hospital bed, as I fight to recover from multiple injuries.

I AM the deer.

An Unexplainable Turn of Events

Love turned itself
towards the sun—

learned how to walk
without limp,

never missed
the cane,

not even the nurse.
It unset itself on fire. Threw
the chains on the door

into the basement—
brought me milk in bed, spoke
a different language but still

showed up at my door
without knocking, left its

heavy bags in the kitchen, opened
every window in the house

&
quietly

sat down and ate breakfast.

Holiday Cards with Mom's Ghost

after Matthew Dickman

     Mom asks for a light
and I remind her smoking kills
and she reminds me she's already dead,
clicking on the electric stove.
     Red rings swirl.
She crushes the tip of her Turkish Silver into them
and smoke unspools from her cigarette
like a loose string, like I could snatch it
and the air would unravel.
     At the kitchen table
I'm addressing envelopes,
and I ask Mom for her new address.
     She says: "Orange juice.
Vodka. Library card. The air before it snows."
How come you never visit my grave?" she asks,
but I don't know how to, without hurting her,
say: "Because you're always here!"
     So I say: "Give me a smoke."
She shakes one from the pack,
and I light it with the tip of hers.
Outside it starts to snow, adding a TV static sheen
to the reflections in the sliding glass doors.
     There's me,
seated at the table. Mom stands behind me,
her hand on my head
      as if to play with my hair.

The River of Ancestors

I want to see the Long River.
The bones of my ancestors are there.
While the Siberian winter slopes
down the Long River,
while the crazy wind blows
and swirls all around.
Somebody is walking on a frozen river
as if walking on a straight path.
In all covered by the dead whiteness.
Oh, how I want to see the Long River!

These days, the king of spring comes
from the valley of shadows to color
the lands by the power of flowers,
to color the rivers by the silk of silver.
And what color is the Long River,
my Terra Paterna, my ancestors' land?

In fresh Siberian summers, the forest birds
are watching the boats on the Long River
and listening to the evening siren sounds,
to the boatmen's loud exclamations,
to the fishermen's furious shouts...
but I've never seen

on which side of the Long River
have fallen the sleeping sundowns,
nor where did the clear daybreaks
fall through the autumn smoke.
Before I lose the last of my days,
please, bring me to the Long River,
to the place where
the bones of my ancestors stay.

Kathrynn Axton-Roosevelt is a poet, spoken word artist, Indigenous advocate, and nationally certified Canadian addictions counsellor. She is the author of *Uncultured Girl* (That Writer Kwe Publications, 2017). Her poetry and editorials have been featured on *AllPoetry Spotlight, Bywords, PoetrySuperHighway, Native Hoop Magazine,* and elsewhere. Mrs. Roosevelt is currently located in La Ronge, Saskatchewan; when she is not writing she spends her time supporting and strengthening Indigenous communities while fostering, mentoring, and teaching two free-spirited and unapologetic Indigenous children.

Louise Bierig grew up in the northwestern corner of Pennsylvania and now lives in the southeastern corner. In both corners, she has enjoyed writing as well as growing native fruits and vegetables. She currently leads the Lansdowne Writers' Workshop, grows a small garden, and along with her husband, raises two sons. She has published her work in *Philadelphia Stories, The Philadelphia Inquirer,* Soul Source newsletter, and *Swarthmorean,* and wrote a column for the Lansdowne Fresh Picks newsletter, "The View from Lupine Valley."

Susan Braghieri is a western Australian writer currently working on an historical fiction novel. Her writing often explores family relationships and the impact of grief and loss. Susan is a participant in the Four Centres' Emerging Writers' Program in Perth, and a past fellow at Katharine Susannah Prichard Writers' Centre. https://www.authorsusan.com/

Kim Darlene Brandon is a storyteller, novelist, poet, and activist. She is the founder of the Brooklyn Society Writers Group. Her work is included in their first anthology, *The Dream Catcher's Song.* She is also published in the *Hawaiian Review* and *Peregrine* and hopes to publish her first of five novels, *Baltimore City Blues,* soon.

Marissa Cagan lives in western Massachusetts with her high school sweetheart. She hopes to write a novel someday.

Steven Carr, who lives in Richmond, Va., began his writing career as a military journalist and has had over 250 short stories published internationally in print and online magazines, literary journals and anthologies since June 2016. Two collections of his short stories, *Sand* and *Rain*, have been published by Clarendon House Publications; his third collection of short stories, *Heat*, was published by Czykmate Productions; and his YA collection of stories, *The Tales of Talker Knock*, was published by Clarendon House Publications. His plays have been produced in several states in the US. He has been nominated for a Pushcart Prize twice. His website is https://www.stevecarr960.com/. He is on Twitter @carrsteven960.

Todd Dillard's work has appeared or is forthcoming in numerous publications, including *Best New Poets, Electric Literature, Superstition Review, The Boiler Journal, Nimrod,* and *Split Lip Magazine.* In addition, his work has been nominated for the Best of the Net, Best Small Fictions, and Pushcart anthologies. He received a grant from the Society of Children's Book Writers and Illustrators, and his chapbook, *The Drowned Hymns,* is available from Jeanne Duval Editions.

Gabriel Green is a dual-titled PhD student at Pennsylvania State University, studying English and African-American studies. His work has been featured in *WusGood Black.*

Atar Hadari's *Songs from Bialik: Selected Poems of H.N. Bialik* (Syracuse University Press) was a finalist for the American Literary Translators' Association award, and his debut collection, *Rembrandt's Bible,* was published by Indigo Dreams in 2013. *Lives of the Dead: Poems of Hanoch Levin* was awarded a Pen Translates grant and is out now from Arc Publications. He contributes a monthly verse Bible translation column to *MOSAIC* magazine.

Summer Hardinge's poetry reflects a way of seeing influenced by growing up in rural Virginia, years of teaching high school English and creative writing, traveling, and digging in her Maryland garden. Writing poetry allows her to wrestle with what she finds curious, beautiful, or discomfiting. As a certified Amherst Writers and Artists facilitator, Summer leads workshops in Maryland, Virginia, and southern France. Her poetry has appeared in *Ekphrastic Review, The Rappahannock Review* and *Beltway Poetry Quarterly.*

John Haugh's writing has been published in *Main Street Rag, Notre Dame Magazine, Rat's Ass Review, The Tipton Poetry Review, Driftwood Press, The Wall Street Journal, Kackalack,* and *Roanoke Review.* He won a couple of poetry awards, including Poetry in Plain Sight. Mr. Haugh lives in North Carolina, was a NCAA national champion in fencing, and spent untold hours browsing Powell's City of Books in Oregon when young. He is working on a chapbook that might be titled "Repurposed Ghost Mixtape."

Tim Hawkins has lived and traveled widely throughout North America, Southeast Asia, Europe, and Latin America, where he has worked as a journalist, technical writer, and teacher in international schools. His career also has taken some interesting detours into such posts as salmon cannery slime table worker, stevedore, nose-hair clipper model, and cram school teacher. He has published more than one hundred pieces of poetry and fiction and has been nominated for Best of the Net (2018), the Pushcart Prize (2011, 2017) and Best Microfiction (2018). His poetry collection, *Wanderings at Deadline,* was published in 2012 by Aldrich Press. Find out more at his website: www.timhawkinspoetry.com

Emerson Henry is a New York-born writer and artist living in Portland, Ore. His work has appeared in *Crazyhorse* and is forthcoming in *Emrys Journal* and *Foglifter*.

Ann Howells edited *Illya's Honey* literary journal from 1999 to 2017. Her books are *Under a Lone Star* (Village Books Press) and *Cattlemen and Cadillacs* (Dallas Poets Community Press), an anthology of D/FW poets she edited. Her chapbook, *Softly Beating Wings*, won the William D. Barney Chapbook Contest for 2017 (Blackbead Books). She has recently published poems in *Chiron Review, Slant,* and *Perfume River,* and a book of Chesapeake Bay poems.

Bisi Ideraabdullah is an activist, educator, and writer. Founder of Imani House, www.imanihouse.org, and the Women of Color Writers' Workshop, she's completing her memoir, "How Many Days Until Tomorrow."

Dena Igusti is an Indonesian-Muslim poet. She is currently the co-founder of Short Line!, an organization dedicated to connecting artists to their communities, to each other, to resources, and to themselves. She is a 2018 NYC Youth Poet Laureate Ambassador and 2017 Urban Word Federal Hall fellow. Her work has been featured in BOAAT Press, *The Shanghai Literary Review,* and more. Find more of her work at denaigusti.wordpress.com.

John Jajeh was born and raised in Atlanta, Ga. He is a student in computer science at Georgia Tech and enjoys writing poetry in his free time. His previous publications include: "Anti-Music Music" in *The North Avenue Review* and "Galaxy of the Sublime (A Sestina)" in *Dark River Review.*

Sam Kealhofer is obtaining a master's degree in English at Mississippi State University. He plans to pursue an MFA.

Andrew Lafleche uses a spoken style of language to blend social criticism, philosophical reflection, explicit prose, and black comedy. His work has appeared in *Alt-Minds, Barren, Bywords, Garfield Lake Review, Gargoyle, Havik, Layman's Way, Lummox, The Manhattanville Review, Military Experience and the Arts, Montana Mouthful, Night Picnic, Paragon Press, PCC Inscape, The Poet's Haven, Polar Expressions, Raven Chronicles, Royal City Literary Arts Society, Sheila-Na-Gig,* and *Snapdragon.*

Sarah Lao is a student at the Westminster Schools in Atlanta, Ga. She edits for *Evolutions Magazine* and reads for *Polyphony Lit,* and her work has been published or is forthcoming in *Sooth Swarm Journal, Eunoia Review,* and *Inflectionist Review.*

Lauren Licona is an Orlando-born indigenous Latina poet. She is currently based in Boston, Mass., where she is pursuing a BA in writing, literature, and publishing at Emerson College. Her work has been featured in *Essence Literary Magazine* and *Rookie Maga.* She was a finalist in the 2018 FEMS tournament and is representing Emerson College at CUPSI in 2019.

LindaAnn LoSchiavo is completing her second documentary film for TV. Her poetry chapbook *Conflicted Excitement* (Red Wolf Editions) was released in 2018.

Gayle Malloy is a western Australian playwright with plays performed in the USA, United Arab Emirates and Australia. She has been awarded the Todhunter Literary award and the John Joseph Jones prize. As a writer, Gayle loves exploring universal themes and is currently writing her first novel.

Tristan Marajh is first-prize winner in both Stratford Rotary Short Story Competition (Canada) and Free Association Books' Short Fiction Competition (England). His other pieces are published in *The Nashwaak Review, Ricepaper Magazine, The New Engagement, The New Quarterly*, and *Existere Journal*. Born in Trinidad and Tobago, he works for the Markham Public Library near Toronto, Canada, where he resides.

Catherine Marenghi's poem was selected last year by acclaimed poet Richard Blanco as first-place winner of a poetry-writing competition sponsored by *Crossroads* magazine. Her poem won the same contest again this year. Last summer she won first place in a poetry competition sponsored by the Marblehead Festival of the Arts in Marblehead, Ma. She won first prize—twice—in the Academy of American Poets University and College Poetry Prize program at Tufts University. Her work has been published in poetry journals both in the US and Mexico, most recently in *Crossroads, Solamente en San Miguel, Italian Americana*, and *Mobius*.

Diane T. Masucci is working in historical fiction. A former journalist, she writes short stories and essays and lives in Montclair, N.J.

Erica McLean is a writer from western Massachusetts with two children in a committed and close relationship with her mom.

Devon Miller-Duggan has published poems in *Rattle, Margie, Christianity and Literature, Gargoyle, Massachusetts Review*, and *Spillway*. She teaches poetry writing at the University of Delaware. Her books include *Pinning the Bird to the Wall* (Tres Chicas Books, 2008), and *Alphabet Year* (Wipf & Stock, 2017). Her chapbook about the aftermath of a Marine's death in Afghanistan, *The Slow Salute*, won the Lithic Press Chapbook Competition (2018).

Michelle Morouse is a pediatrician in Pontiac, Mich. Her poems and flash fiction have appeared, or will appear, in *The Journal of Compressed Creative Arts, Third Wednesday, The MacGuffin, The Light Ekphrastic*, and *Oxford Magazine*, among others.

Molly Murray is the outdoor editor of *Panorama*, the journal of Intelligent Travel and the author of *Today, She Is* (Wipf & Stock, 2014). Her essays, stories, and poetry have appeared in *Panorama, Litro, Ruminate, The Quarterday Review, The Laurel Review, The Wayfarer, The Windhover, From Glasgow to Saturn, Ink, Sweat & Tears,* and many others. One of her poems is nominated for a 2019 Pushcart Prize. Molly has an MLit in creative writing from the University of Glasgow and a certificate in creative writing from the University of Oxford Department of Continuing Education.

Elena Naskova is a published poet and playwright who writes plays, haiku, and free-form poems. Her plays have been performed all over the USA and in a few places abroad.

Stephen O'Donnell is a writer living in Dublin, Ireland. His short stories have appeared in *The Bloody Key Society, Five on the Fifth, Gambling the Aisle,* and *The Avalon Literary Review,* among other publications.

David S. Osgood is a short-story writer. He resides in Holly Springs, N.C., where rural and suburban collide among crepe myrtles. David has a BA in creative writing from the University of Southern California. He has been recently published in *Open: Journal of Arts & Letters, Crack the Spine, Firewords, Treehouse,* and *Eastern Iowa Review,* won the Microfiction Honorable Mention award from San Antonio Writer's Guild, and is gratefully awaiting additional publication in *Mulberry Fork Review* and *Glassworks.*

OyaBisi, see Bisi Iderabdullah.

Hannah Pelletier studied English at the University of New Hampshire, where she received the Richard M. Ford writing award two years in a row. Her work has been published in *The Paragon Journal, Split Rock Review, Remembered Arts Journal, Thin Air Mag,* and more. Hannah is a twenty-four-year-old expat living in Paris.

C. Platt is a poet and freelance writer/editor who lives in Northampton, Mass., with her teenaged children. She attends Mount Holyoke College as a Frances Perkins scholar and works for Interlink publishing.

Alena Podobed is an author from Russia. Diploma-teacher of history and social science, he is a member of the union of artists and has worked more than twenty years as a graphic designer. He has been writing poetry and prose since 2006. He is the author of the collection (poetry and prose) *Carousel for the Fool* and has publications in numerous almanacs.

Leslie Blackman Poulin is a graduate of Vermont College of Fine Arts where she earned an MFA in poetry. She studied poetry in Greece as an undergraduate and in Slovenia as a graduate student. She was nominated by faculty for the Best New Poets competition in 2015, and her work is forthcoming in *The MacGuffin.* Leslie has lived in Maine her whole life and has been writing poetry since she was a child. She lives in South Portland where she enjoys gardening, creating art, and working on her first love, poetry.

Laurie Rosen lives by the coast in Massachusetts and makes frequent trips to a Vermont home tucked deep into a hollow. She is inspired by travel, nature, politics, and the myriad photographs she takes of her surroundings. Her poems have appeared in *Sisyphus, Tigershark Magazine*, and *Beach Reads*, an anthology from Third Street Writers.

Sandip Saha is a chemical engineer and has a PhD in metallurgical engineering from India. He received three awards for his scientific work and has published thirty-three pieces on his scientific research work, including three patents. He is a winner of Poetry Matters Project Lit Prize and has published one collection of poems (anthology), *Quest for Freedom*, available in Amazon.com. He is published in many poetry journals, including *Better Than Starbucks Poetry Magazine, Pif Magazine, The Cape Rock: Poetry, Las Positas Anthology-Havik, Pasadena City College Inscape Magazine, VerbalArt, Phenomenal Literature, India, The Pangolin Review, North Dakota Quarterly* and *The Wayne Literary Review*.

Jamie Samdahl is a poet and naturalist from rural Massachusetts. Her poems have appeared in *Rattle, Washington Square Review, Mountain Record: The Zen Practitioners' Journal*, and elsewhere. In 2013 John Yao, Mary Jo Salter, and Cleopatra Matthis named Jamie winner of the 90th Annual Glascock Poetry Contest. An environmentalist as much as a writer, Jamie has worked as a national park ranger in Colorado, Nevada, and California.

Jake Sandler's work has appeared in *IthacaLit* and elsewhere.

Joyce Schmid's recent poetry has appeared in *Poetry Daily, Missouri Review, New Ohio Review, Antioch Review*, and other journals and anthologies. She lives in Palo Alto, Calif., with her husband of over half a century.

Peter Schneider is a poet who has also been a farmer, theologian, co-director of Amherst Writers & Artists, and father of four children. A Wisconsin native. he lives in Amherst, Mass., and has been married to his best friend for sixty-two years. Peter's book of poems, *Line Fence,* includes poems about memory loss that are being widely used among those caring for, and experiencing, memory loss. Another book of his poems is forthcoming from AWA Press.

Maureen Sherbondy's work has appeared *in Southeast Review, Stone Canoe, The Cortland Review, Prelude,* and other journals. She teaches English at Alamance Community College in North Carolina. Her forthcoming book of poems, *Dancing with Dali*, will be published in 2020.

Horacio Sierra was born and raised in Miami, Fla. He earned a BS in communication from the University of Miami and a PhD in English from the University of Florida. He splits his time between Miami and Washington, DC.

Dorsia Smith Silva is a full professor of English at the University of Puerto Rico, Río Piedras, and her poems have been published in *Aji Magazine, Gravel, MORIA Literary Magazine, Tipton Poetry Journal, Penultimate Peanut Magazine, Snapdragon: A Journal of Art and Healing, Edison Literary Review, Apple Valley Review, Bright Sleep Magazine, Foliate Oak Literary Magazine, The B'K, WINK, Poetry Quarterly, POUI: Cave Hill Journal of Creative Writing,*

Adanna, Rigorous, Shot Glass Journal, Tonguas, and in the book *Mothers and Daughters.*

Rose Strode is a poet and essayist. Her work has been published in *The Gettysburg Review, Poet Lore, The Delmarva Review, Little Patuxent Review, Waxwing,* and *The Broad River Review,* among others. She attended George Mason University in the poetry MFA program, is a recipient of the 2018-19 Gulick Fellowship through Valpariso University, and is a volunteer gardener at a Buddhist temple.

Jessica Thornton is a student at the University of South Florida majoring in English and advertising. Her poetic life is greatly influenced by some of her favorite poets, including Kaveh Akbar, Safia Elhillo, Wendy Xu, and Tracy K. Smith. In spite of what seems to be a late-onset lactose intolerance, her favorite ice cream flavor is cookie dough. She has previously been published in *Thread,* USF's undergrad literary journal.

Slavica Turinski-Lazić is a Croatian poet, prose writer, and painter. In 2016 the publishing house Nova POETIKA (Belgrade, Republic of Serbia) published her poetry collection *Lineage of Twilight,* collected by the Serbian National Library. Her poems and stories have appeared in numerous anthologies in the former Yugoslavia, as well as in *The Grief Diaries, The Bangalore Review, River River Journal,* and *Literary Orphans Journal.* In 2017 the Poets House from New York City selected her poem for the Master Class with Kazim Ali. She lives and works in Slavonia and Baranya (Croatia).

Pam Vap is an eighteen-year English teacher living on the plains of Nebraska. She was the recipient of the Outstanding Thesis Award from University of Nebraska at Kearney for "Nightwriting: A Collection of Poetry, and Reflections on the Creative Process." In addition, she was a first-place Goodreads poetry contest winner and was awarded first place in the 2018 "Cultural Integration on the High Plains" poetry contest.

Two of **Matt Vevakis'** poems are being set to music for the renowned Quorum Boston—a twenty-person vocal ensemble focused on promoting LGBTQ-plus voices.

Silver Webb is a fiction writer and poet living in California who recently had a story published in *Santa Barbara Literary Journal* (June 2018), and one in the *Hurricane & Swan Songs* anthology (April 2019).

Vanessa Williams is a twenty-six-year-old mother of two who loves writing to encourage, teach, and help others.

Nicole Zdeb is a writer based in Portland, Ore. She holds an MFA from Iowa Writers' Workshop and volunteers as the development director for Twilight Theater Company.

Peregrine

THE JOURNAL OF AMHERST WRITERS & ARTISTS

Peregrine has provided a forum for national and international writers since 1983, and is committed to finding exceptional work by both emerging and established writers. We seek work that is unpretentious, memorable, and reflects diversity of voice. We accept only original and unpublished poetry and short stories. No work for or by children. *Peregrine*, published by Amherst Writers & Artists Press, is staffed by volunteers. All decisions are made by the editors after all submissions have arrived, so our response time may be slower than that of other literary journals. We welcome simultaneous submissions.

Poetry: Three to five single-spaced, one-page poems. We seek poems that inform and surprise us.

Prose: Short stories, double-spaced, 750 words maximum (include word count on first page); shorter stories have a better chance.

For additional submission details, please see www.amherstwriters.com or peregrinejournal.submittable.com. All submissions are via submittable.com unless other arrangements are made.

Additional copies of this issue are available at Amazon.com for $12.

The Editors
Amherst Writers & Artists Press
P.O. Box 1076
Amherst, MA 01004
www.amherstwriters.org

Death & sex =
Both take us to
infinite unknown
spaces = we cry,
we float —
        we cry,
        we ~~are~~, float
we dance with the
~~wind~~ — Our body
unknown
is weightless =
        we cry
        we float
we're in unknown
space —
                    2/26/2020

Made in the USA
Middletown, DE
10 January 2020